the art of
UND
ACHIEVE
MENT

Demotivational, Uninspirational & Disappointing Affirmations and Wisdom – for the Average

COLORING BOOK
for adults

it's okay to just be okay!

Maxwell Easeley

ISBN 9798884409552

Notice to Readers:

Welcome to the world of humor and satire presented in this book. Before you embark on this journey of laughter and merriment, please take a moment to understand the nature of this content: _Satirical Content_: This book is a work of satire, intended solely for entertainment purposes. It's akin to a literary whoopee cushion, designed to induce laughter and amusement. _Not Professional Advice_: The content herein does not constitute professional advice of any kind, be it medical, therapeutic, or life coaching. It is purely for fun and should not be taken seriously. _Discretion Advised_: If you find the humor or content inappropriate or not to your taste, please exercise your discretion. This book might not be suitable for all audiences. _No Practical Implementation_: The ideas, jokes, and content in this book are not meant to be implemented or acted upon. They are for reading enjoyment only. It's a source of laughter, not a guide for action. _Financial Limitation of Liability_: We, the author(s) and publisher(s) of this book, hold zero financial responsibility for any outcomes, direct or indirect, resulting from the interpretation or use of the contents of this book. This includes any form of financial compensation or reimbursement. _Use at Your Own Risk_: Any attempt to apply or enact scenarios or suggestions from this book is entirely at the reader's risk. The author(s) and publisher(s) assume no responsibility for any consequences that may arise from such actions.

By continuing to read and enjoy this book, you, as the reader, acknowledge and accept this disclaimer, recognizing the book's purpose as a source of humor and acknowledging the financial limitation of liability.

Enjoy the read, but remember – it's meant to tickle your funny bone, not to guide your life decisions.

Dive into a world where mediocrity is not just accepted; it's celebrated!

"The Art of Underachievement Coloring Book: Embrace Your Mediocre Palette" is the perfect companion to the hilariously demotivational "The Art of Underachievement – Embracing Mediocrity in a World Obsessed with Success."

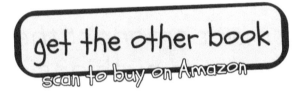 

Designed for the average, the unambitious, and everyone in between, these books take the art of underachievement to a whole new level

whatever you do, just remember it's OK to just be OK!
Maxwell Easeley

the art of
UNDER ACHIEVE MENT ☺

podcast

Let's meet amongst the comfortable cushions and soft sofas of not-so-mediocre **podcast platforms**.

Search for _The Art of Underachievement by Maxwell Easeley_

Test your average colors and your mediocre skills here

on Amazon Music, Spotify, Apple Podcasts, and more

the art of
UNDER
ACHIEVE
MENT ː)

podcast

Practicing mediocrity coloring yet?

PUTTING IN MAXIMUM EFFORT MEANS MORE THINGS CAN GO WRONG.

AIM FOR 'JUST ENOUGH'.

Float in the tranquil sea of aimlessness, where the waves of failure never crash.

on Amazon Music, Spotify, Apple Podcasts, and more

the art of
UNDER ACHIEVE MENT ☺
podcast

Let's meet amongst the comfortable cushions and soft sofas of not-so-mediocre **podcast platforms**.

Search for _The Art of Underachievement by Maxwell Easeley_

EMBRACE THE FLOW OF LIFE'S STREAM

let each binge wash over you like a gentle wave.

Your comfort zone

Where dreams gently expire, so you don't have to chase them.

WHY FINISH WHAT YOU START WHEN YOU CAN SAVOR THE MYSTERY OF WHAT COULD HAVE BEEN?

Let every snooze be a silent rebellion against the dawn of productivity.

Wage war on the morning alarm; your bed, the trench, and sleep, your ally in RESISTANCE.

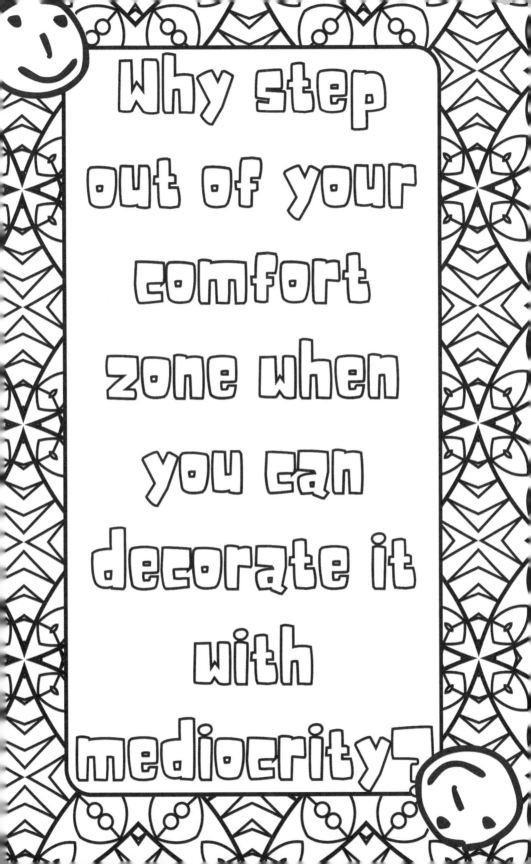

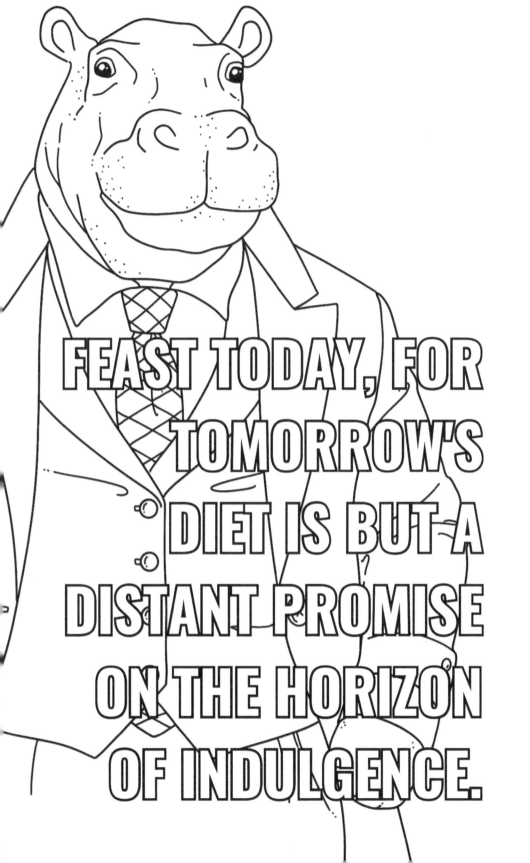

Stretching your limits is a risk. Embrace the safety of the familiar pillow fort.

Let life unfold in episodes; savor the pause between seasons as much as the cliffhangers.

In the quest for
enlightenment,
may your feed
BE ENDLESS
and
your battery,
ETERNAL.

the art of

UNDER ACHIEVE MENT ☺

podcast

Let's meet amongst the comfortable cushions and soft sofas of not-so-mediocre **podcast platforms**.

Search for *The Art of Underachievement by Maxwell Easeley*

IN THE ART OF LIVING, A MESSY BED IS A MASTERPIECE PAINTED DAILY WITH THE STROKES OF REST.

IN THE QUIET OF UNSCHEDULED EVENINGS, FIND BLISS IN THE COMPANY OF YOUR OWN SOLITUDE.

EMBRACE THE ETERNAL CYCLE OF UNRESTED SHEETS: TODAY'S CREASES ARE TOMORROW'S COMFORT.

IN THE GARDEN OF
EXISTENCE, LET
YOUR PATH BE
GUIDED BY THE WIND,
NOT BY MARKERS OF
AMBITION.

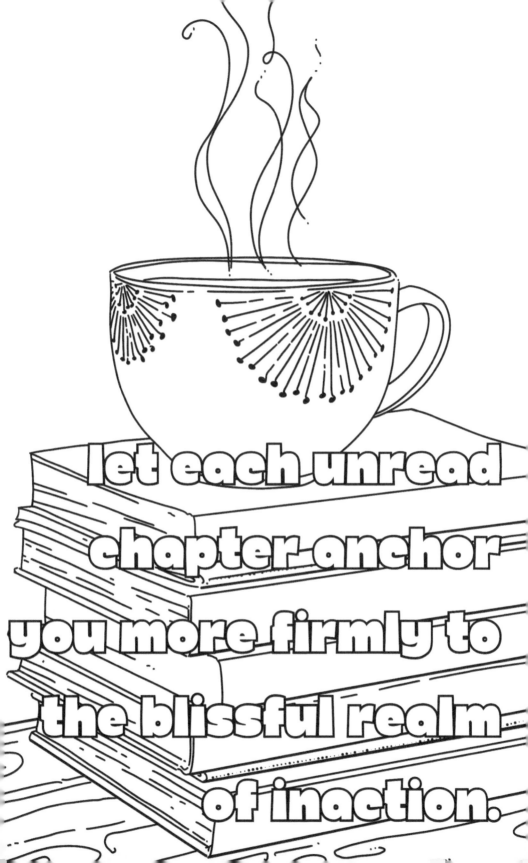

let each unread chapter anchor you more firmly to the blissful realm of inaction.

IN THE CALENDAR OF SELF-IMPROVEMENT, TOMORROW IS A RECURRING DAY OF HOPEFUL BEGINNINGS.

IN THE CHORUS OF LIFE,
THERE'S HARMONY IN
BEING ANOTHER VOICE,
NOT ALWAYS THE SOLO.

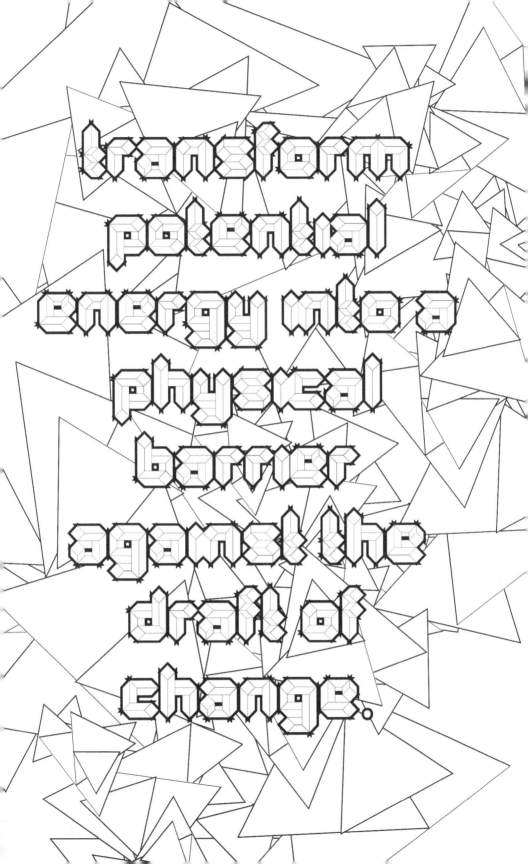

transform potential energy into a physical barrier against the draft of change.

CULTIVATE A GARDEN OF MODEST DREAMS, WHERE THE FRUITS OF REALITY ARE ALWAYS WITHIN REACH.

SAVOR THE PRESENT: TOMORROW'S RESTRAINT IS JUST ANOTHER DESSERT AWAY.

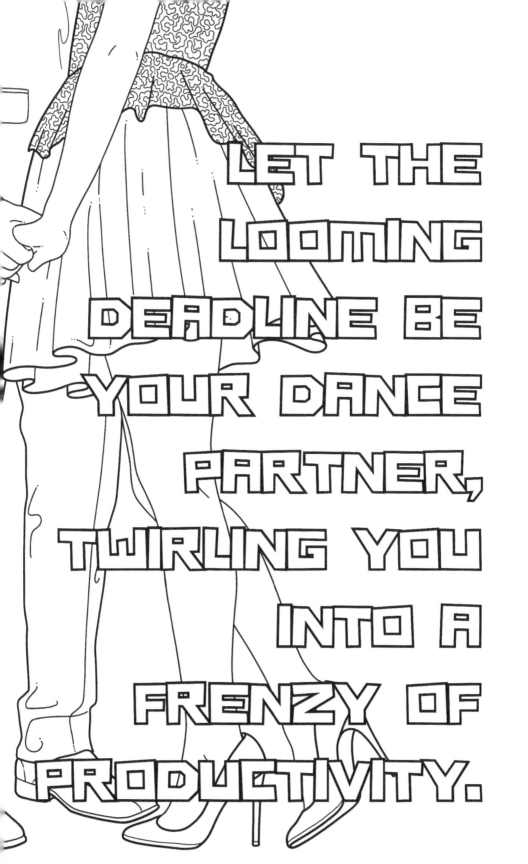

Embrace the adrenaline of the eleventh hour, where inspiration rushes in with the ticking clock.

HARNESS THE WEIGHT OF WISDOM TO HOLD OPEN THE DOOR TO YOUR COMFORTABLY STAGNANT ROOM.

Made in United States
Troutdale, OR
05/10/2024

19782966R00066